Vol. 1456

JOHANN SEBASTIAN BACH

Eight Little Preludes and Fugues

Of the First Master-Period

For the Organ

A Critico-Practical Edition by

CHARLES - MARIE WIDOR and ALBERT SCHWEITZER

With Hammond Registration

ISBN: 978-0-7935-7287-8

G. SCHIRMER, Inc.

DISTRIBUTED BY

7777 W. BLUEMOUND RD. P.O. BOX 13819 MILWAUKEE, WI 53213

Contents

Literary and Critical Notes

All the compositions in this volume have been preserved only in copies.

The fugues and preludes in this volume belong to Bach's earlier Master-period. He has entered his individual path, but in the form appears still dependent on German and Italian models.

An exact dating of the several pieces is impossible; but it may be assumed that they all originated during Bach's sojourn in Arnstadt, Mühlhausen and Weimar, that is to say, between the years 1704 and 1717. It is likely, however, that the period of their inception was much shorter, for the works belonging to the later years at Weimar (where Bach labored 1708–17) display a much greater maturity of form. We are probably safe in assuming that these numbers were all composed previous to the year 1714.

The eight short preludes were intended for instructive pieces. It is quite possible that they have been handed down to us, not in their original shape, but rewritten with emendations. This supposition most plausibly explains the fact that they exhibit traits of a certain imperfection side by side with masterly writing. The revision may have been done at the time when Bach was initiating his oldest sons into the organist's art with the aid of these preludes and fugues.

A spontaneous vivacity of invention lends to the works of the First Master-Period an especial charm. Of all Bach's organ pieces, their appeal to the hearer is perhaps the most elemental, and the interpreter will always experience something of the effect which the Master himself must have felt when he brought out in these pieces, for the first time, everything in wealth of tone and possibility of combination that the organ could yield.

CH.-M. WIDOR, *Paris*.   A. SCHWEITZER, *Strassburg*.

Suggestions for Performing the Preludes and Fugues of the First Master-Period

Preliminary Observations

The remarks on the interpretation of the several preludes and fugues will be strictly limited to a statement of formulas.

The directions are calculated, in most cases, for a two-manual organ. For the preludes and fugues Bach generally employed only his great-manual and his *Rückpositiv* (choir), his third manual not being sufficiently full-toned to be used on a level with the other two. On the earlier organs an alternation between choir and swell could not well be considered, because the great-manual lay between them. It is certain that all the Master's works can be performed on a well-arranged and finely-voiced two-manual instrument in a correct and wholly appropriate manner.

For a number of preludes and fugues, however, our "suggestions" are intended to be carried out on a three-manual organ. But the directions may be transferred without difficulty to one having only two rows of keys.

In a two-manual organ, Man. II should be in the swell-box; in a three-manual organ, Man. III.

All manuals are supposed to be provided with good foundation stops, compound stops ("mixtures") and reeds. The swell-organ should be abundantly furnished with stops of all classes. The effect obtained by opening and closing the shutters should be such as to make itself felt when the swell-manual is coupled to the great and the hands are playing on the latter.

In its relation to the instrument as a whole, the swell-organ should impart flexibility and a capacity for modulating the tone-effects.

The Fifth, Twelfth, etc., are reckoned among the foundation stops; Thirds and Sevenths, and their octaves, are to be used with the compound stops.

For the arrangement of the combination or composition pedals, pistons, etc., and of the couplers, the suggestions of the International Regulations for Organ-building have been adopted as drafted by the committee headed by Dr. Albert Schweitzer and Abbé Dr. Xavier Mathias. The couplers and auxiliaries above mentioned should be workable either by hand or by foot, as occasion serves.

The player is not expected to use the ordinary *crescendo*-pedals, which bring on the stops in a succession fixed beforehand.

The suggestions can be carried out, in general, only with the aid of an assistant for drawing or retiring the stops at the proper place. This was the method adopted by Bach himself when he wished to shade his registration with special care.

Should the player prefer to make the changes in registration himself, with the help of modern appliances, he may simplify our suggestions accordingly by drawing or retiring his stops in groups where the editors propose to bring them on or retire them successively.

The decisive factor is not the arrangements for facilitating registration — for in Bach-playing these may frequently be replaced to advantage by an assistant — but the tone produced. Your instrument must have at command fine, clear-voiced stops, neither too dull nor too blaring. The foundation stops, mixtures and reeds, when combined, must produce a *forte* through which the polyphony can be clearly traced, and which does not weary the ear.

For such an ideal instrument, which any good organ-builder can construct if allowed the means and the time, the Editors' suggestions are calculated. They afford merely general indications as to place and direction in which an alteration of timbre or a change of manual is to be effected. It remains for the organist to fit these formulas to the instrument on which he has to play.

For instance, when choir and swell are not provided with good mixtures, the effect which the Editors propose to obtain on the ideal organ by drawing or retiring these registers will have to be realized by the use of foundation stops, more especially those of four-foot or two-foot tone, by coupling and uncoupling the manuals, or in some other suitable manner.

When some of the foundation stops are too dull or too harsh in tone, they should not be employed in every case where the Editors suppose all the foundation stops (eight-, four- and two-foot) to be drawn. On the other hand, you may draw one or another of these stops as a substitute (but only in case of need) for a missing mixture stop.

Unfortunately, a good interpretation of Bach's organ works depends not alone on the artistic quality of the player, but also on that of the instrument. Organists of all nationalities should, therefore, see to it that in cathedrals, village churches and concert-halls only simple, substantial, finely-voiced and full-toned instruments are set up, to the end that coming generations may find it easier to play Bach well than our own, in which far too many organists are condemned, by the defects of organs built according to wrong principles, to an incomplete interpretation of the Master's works.

The better the instrument, the fewer will be the needful readjustments of the Editors' indications.

Respecting the reinforcement and reduction of the pedal by drawing and retiring stops and couplers, the Notes contain hints only in exceptional cases, it being assumed that the pedal will follow the manuals with a suitable volume of tone [suitable bass!].

Suggestions for the intercoupling and uncoupling of the manuals are also seldom made. In this matter the player will be governed by the special arrangements of his instrument and the relations subsisting between the several manuals with regard to volume and quality of tone.

Of course, directions for using the swell are also given only in passages of special prominence.

The Editors have been particularly careful to indicate, as precisely as possible, the way in which a change of manual is to be effected, wherever it occurs, as a great deal depends upon this.

Wherever a phrasing is proposed, the "ideal" phrasing is intended, which shows the player how the phrase is to be understood and conceived. It will depend on his own artistic sense, the quality of the voicing of his organ and its keyboard facilities, how closely he can approximate the ideal phrasing in the audible interpretation.

The "breathing-mark" (') indicates a noticeable "lift" (break). Inserted between notes which are repeated in the same part, it signifies that they are to be sustained for only half their time-value.

Short slurs included under one long one ⌒⌒⌒ show the units which combine to form a period or figure. They should be set off by brief, hardly perceptible breaks.

Tenuto-dashes under a slur ‿ _ _ ‿ call for a sort of free *legato* in which the notes are not smoothly connected, but slightly separated. In reality, such tones will frequently have to be played in an ordinary *legato*, as the organ does not control the more delicate nuances between *tenuto* and *legato*.

Notes marked with the simple *tenuto*-dashes, without a slur, are to be separated. They should be sustained for the greater part of their time-value, the key being allowed to rise just before the next key is depressed, so that an extremely brief break results.

During the progress of their work it has become increasingly evident to the Editors that the Notes have, on the whole, a tendency toward sketchiness. In many cases they had to content themselves with mere hints, instead of going into details; other points, which should have been reasoned out, had to be stated as simple assertions; and some more or less plausible alternative readings could not be mentioned at all.

Any one who realizes the difficulties encountered in concisely explaining the musical processes involved in the interpretation of preludes and fugues will be indulgent toward the present attempt — the first ever made in this direction; in forming his opinions he will strive to penetrate the artistic thought of the Editors, and to associate himself with them in spirit as they, during their arduous common labors, were associated and felt themselves at one with each other and with other known and unknown colleagues, near or far. Such association is always found where men meet in a common striving after perfection, and hear a voice saying: "Put off thy shoes from off thy feet, for the place whereon thou standest is holy ground," and feel that in being permitted to touch the sacred instrument and set forth the works of Johann Sebastian Bach a blessing has entered into their lives.

Eight Little Preludes and Fugues

I. Prelude and Fugue in C Major. (Pages 2-5.)

PRELUDE

In this piece Bach did not provide for any change of manual, for the pedal-part is continuous from beginning to end. It is a question, if the registration should exhibit much variety. Many players will be unable to withstand the temptation to work up the augmentations extending throughout both divisions of the piece by drawing additional registers. When this is done, begin with the foundation stops of the coupled manuals, and from the fifth measure onward gradually add mixtures and reeds. With measure 13, throw off the mixtures and reeds of the great organ, and close the swell-box. By opening this latter through measures 15–19 a natural *crescendo* will be brought out. Following this, bring on the mixtures and reeds of the great-organ.

But the Prelude has a much better effect when played in a fine, unchanging *forte* — whether with or without reeds, we shall not decide — from beginning to close, or at most by indicating the shading with the swell, when the instrument permits of so doing.

A student, initiated into Bach's art of organ-playing with this piece, should learn from it that the effect depends, above all, on a quiet, clear and cleanly phrased style of playing.

The phrasing, in accordance with which the second, third and fourth sixteenth-notes in each beat are joined in a group with the first sixteenth-note of the next beat, must be carried out consistently, but with extreme discretion, in order that the student may, in his first Prelude, become acquainted with the fundamental problem of Bach-playing on the organ — the phrasing within the *legato* without interrupting the latter. He ought equally to realize that all directions for phrasing bear but a crude resemblance to that which his inner vision and hearing reveal, and which he should realize with his fingers.

FUGUE

Concerning the Fugue there may be a doubt as to whether the two episodes (from the third eighth-note before the end of measure 12 to the first in measure 16, and from the third eighth-note before the end of measure 20 to the first in measure 22) might not be played on Manual II. Despite the brevity of the two sections in question, the changes of manual have a good effect. Of course, on the second eighth-note in measure 22 one goes over to the great-manual with the right hand only, keeping both inner parts on Manual II until the entrance of the pedal.

Should you wish to bring out the effect of augmentation by means of registration, add stops to the great during the episodes on the choir. But one may also draw, at the very beginning, the foundation stops of the whole organ (without the 16-foot manual stops), as well as the mixtures, and leave this registration unaltered to the close.

Some organists registrate as follows: They begin with the foundation stops; on the third eighth-note before the end of measure 12 they draw the mixtures, still remaining on the great-manual; on the third eighth-note before the end of measure 20, they also add the reeds.

II. Prelude and Fugue in D Minor. (Pages 6-9.)

PRELUDE

Begin the Prelude on the great-manual. On the third eighth-note in measure 7 go over to the choir, and remain on it until the third eighth-note in measure 12. If your organ has three manuals, the right hand may play on the swell, the left on the choir. The swell-box closes slowly, so that the episode runs on in a gradual *decrescendo*.

With the final eighth-note in measure 12, return to the great-manual, and remain there up to the first eighth-note in the third beat of measure 20. From here till the beginning of the runs in sixteenths in measure 23, stay on the choir-manual; then go back to the great, and remain there to the close.

No change in the registration is required. The piece can be played through to the end with the foundation stops and mixtures of the great- and choir-manuals. But if variety be desired, the mixtures may be thrown off at the return to the great-manual in measure 12; then proceed at first with only foundation stops, and bring on the retired mixtures gradually in the course of the following measures to work up the augmentation.

For the return to the great-manual in measure 23, reeds may be added if desired. Then, during the runs in measures 23 and 24, still more stops may be added, so that on the first beat of measure 25 the full organ enters.

In case the piece is played as an interlude, it should be performed with a selection of fine foundation stops, the *crescendi* and *decrescendi* being brought out by the aid of the swell.

FUGUE

The first ten measures are played on the great-manual. From the last eighth-note in measure 10 to the second quarter in measure 17, play on Manual II.

From the last eighth-note in measure 20 to the reëntry of the pedal, alternate between Man. I and Man. II, going over to Man. II on the last eighth-note in measure 20, returning to Man. I on the last eighth-note in measure 21, again going over to Man. II on the last eighth-note in measure 22, and finally returning to Man. I on the last eighth-note in measure 23.

During the above-named measures some players always keep the inner parts on Manual II, and alternate only with the soprano. But the effect is finer when all the parts alternate together.

Opinions differ as to the way in which the change of manual should be effected at the transition from measure 10 to measure 11. It seems to be generally agreed that the inner parts should go over to Man. II with the second quarter in measure 11. On the other hand, it is a moot point whether the highest part should already go over on the last eighth-note in measure 10, or if it would not be better to keep it for a while on the great-manual, not making the change until the sustained *F*, that is, on the first beat of measure 12.

This transition is very effective, but rather difficult of execution on our broad-scale keyboards, as the last eighth-note in the alto in measure 11 must be taken with the right hand on Man. II while the same hand is still holding down the *F* on the great-manual. On the keyboard of Bach's time even a hand of medium size could take both the inner parts on the second manual.

The swell-box closes during the course of measures 12 and 13, again opening through measures 16 and 17.

The return to the great-manual at the entrance of the pedal can be effected by carrying over both hands together on the third quarter of measure 17. But it sounds better when the tenor part alone makes the transition at that place, letting the two higher parts follow after in the middle of measure 18; the soprano on the second eighth-note of the second beat, the alto on the third quarter.

The Fugue should be played with foundation stops, either alone or with mixtures added. If you desire to bring on an augmentation, embrace the opportunity in measures 20–23 while the hands are on the second manual to reinforce the great-organ. In any event, the degree of tone-power in which the close is to be made must be reached with the entrance of the pedal in measure 26.

III. Prelude and Fugue in E Minor. (Pages 10-12.)

PRELUDE

The most natural style of interpretation for this wonderful Prelude is to play it throughout on the great-organ in a fine, even-toned *forte*. Should one prefer to bring out the intensification by adding stops, this may best be done on the third quarter in measure 9, the second eighth in measure 11, the first quarter in measure 15, and between the first and second quarters of measure 18. Some organists may, however, think it better to play the section from the second eighth-note in measure 11 to the corresponding point in measure 15 with more subdued tone than what precedes and follows. But as a general thing it is preferable, just in this Prelude, that the student should make the intensification felt, not by means of the registration, but by the clarity in development and the convincing power of his interpretation. By dint of striving to master the difficulties inherent in a plastic development of the phrasing of this polyphony, he will find a full reward and take genuine pleasure in this composition.

FUGUE

It is not easy to settle the alternation of manuals for the Fugue. A good effect is obtained by going over to the second manual with the inner parts on the second quarter of measure 45, keeping the soprano on the great-manual till the first quarter in measure 48, and returning to the latter with the two highest parts on the second eighth-note in measure 54, the tenor following them on the next eighth.

Some players like to go over to the second manual as early as measure 28, in doing which they first take the two inner parts on the great-manual, and then (on the second beat) take them on the choir; while in the pedal they employ, up to measure 46, only 8-foot registers.

Other players prefer to do without any change of manual whatever in this fugue, conceiving the piece as flowing on in one continuous augmentation, which they endeavor to bring out by adding registers on the first quarter of measure 28, the first quarter of measure 39, and the first quarter of measure 54.

Another alternative is imaginable, in which, while equally rejecting a change of manuals, the player retires registers in measures 28, 39 and 45 (or throws off the manual couplers), returning to the original tone-power only with measure 54.

Opinions are likewise divided with regard to the registration. Ought we to play the fugue with foundation stops alone, or may we also employ mixtures and reeds during its course? The decision depends on our conception of the theme, some leaning toward a lyrical interpretation, while others incline to a loftier characterization.

IV. Prelude and Fugue in F Major. (Pages 13-16.)

PRELUDE

In the Prelude the learner may revel his fill in changing manuals and registration. It is developed like an aria. Between two identical main sections — measures 1–14 and 45–58 — an episode is interpolated. The two main sections must, of course, be contrasted with the episode through their similar heavier registration.

We propose, by way of example, the following *modus operandi*, which may be shaped in more simple or complex fashion according to the player's will or need.

For the introduction and the finale there should be drawn, on Manual I. Diapasons and Gambas; on Manual II, Diapasons and Flutes. The manuals are coupled together. The right hand plays on Manual II, the left on Manual I.

On the second sixteenth-note in measure 12, and again in measure 56, the right hand may go over to the great-manual for the closing cadence. The inner parts entering in the above-named measures must, of course, be played on the great-manual.

For the middle section the manuals are uncoupled. On Manual I retain only string-tone; on Manual II, only Flutes. In measures 15–18, 23–28, and 35–44 the right hand plays on Manual I, the left on Manual II; for measures 19–22, and 29–34 the left hand is on Manual II, the right on Manual I. From measure 35 onward the two manuals are again coupled together; on the second sixteenth-note of measure 42 the right hand also goes over to the great-manual.

Where three manuals are at one's disposal, still greater variety can be introduced into the episode. In particular, one should employ the Gambas and Salicionals enclosed in the swell-box of Manual III.

This is likewise an excellent practice-piece for learning how to operate the swell-pedal. Of course, the swell is open during introduction and finale, and also while playing measures 15–18; it closes during the course of measures 19–22, opens during measures 23–28, and then stays open to measure 34. Before measure 35 it is closed *subito*, thereafter opening again slowly until measure 44 is reached.

The student may find a different employment of the swell preferable to the one proposed. But he should clearly understand that whatever he undertakes to do with the swell-pedal must not be left to the inspiration of the moment, but maturely considered and carefully tried out beforehand.

The experience won by practice will familiarize him with the fact that the unrestful feeling engendered by a liberal use of the swell-pedal and a frequent change of manuals can be banished only by the even balance of a delicately shaded tempo.

Manifestly, this Prelude may also be played far more simply; and when treated thus it will appear to gain rather than to lose in effect.

FUGUE

The Fugue comes out best when played from beginning to end on the great-organ with foundation stops alone, or with mixtures added. A player desiring a sustained *crescendo* will frequently find good opportunities to add stops from measure 15 onward. As such we may point out the last eighth-note in measure 15, the rest in measure 22, the rests in measures 23 and 24, and the fourth eighth-note in measure 25.

The student should learn to make his choice of these possibilities. He should also attempt, at the end of measure 15, to transfer to the second manual, so as to make a thorough test of the difficulties met with in returning to the great-

manual, as demanded by the subsequent entrance of the pedal. It is advisable, in so doing, to let the tenor part go over to the great-manual on the third eighth-note in measure 18, following with the alto on the second quarter in measure 19, and the soprano on the third quarter.

V. Prelude and Fugue in G Major. (Pages 17-19.)

PRELUDE

Begin the Prelude with the full organ, even the 16-foot registers of the manuals being drawn. On the rest in measure 5, retire the reeds and 16-foot stops, and continue — in case you aim at variety — on the second manual as far as the second sixteenth in measure 9, then going over to the great. Thereafter increase again up to full organ, which should be reached with the entrance of the pedal solo.

The entire movement may, however, be played through from beginning to end on the great-manual with a fine combination of foundation stops, mixtures and reeds.

FUGUE

In the phrasing of the theme, avoid all exaggeration. The "lift" between the second eighth-note on the odd beat and the following quarter-note must be of such brief duration that the hearer is hardly conscious of a break. He should only be made to feel that the player has it in his power, so to speak, to endow the second and fourth quarters with some special accent required by the logical development of the theme.

Or the phrasing may be so conceived that the "lift" is made between the first and second eighth-notes of the odd beats, and the second eighth-note slurred on to the following quarter-note. We should then play like this:

It is hard to decide which of these two phrasings is the better. At bottom, one is as good as the other, for either throws the requisite accent in the same way on to the second and fourth quarter-notes. The first is possibly more characteristic than the second.

At this point the student should familiarize himself with the difficulties in fingering which arise when the player does not content himself with bringing out the phrasing of the theme at its first entry, but endeavors to carry out the same phrasing all through the fugue, and to render it recognizable and audible amid the polyphonic weft solely by means of the accents which he is able to impart to it.

From this fugue he can learn, at the same time, that in Bach-playing the phrasing of the contrapuntal parts, throughout their course, ought to proceed motivewise out of that of the theme. Hence, in measures 18 and 19 and in similar passages one does not play a simple *legato*, as one would do were the fugue not dominated by this theme; but here (as in the principal theme) we lift imperceptibly between the eighth-notes and the following quarter-notes, supposing our first phrasing of the theme to have been chosen.

True, this continual lifting, however discreetly it may be executed, gives the fugue a certain harsh and angular effect; and this will move some players to adopt the second phrasing of the theme, in accordance wherewith measures 18 and 19, and the corresponding passages, are to be played absolutely *legato*.

The student should practise the fugue with both phrasings.

It is evident that we must go over to the second manual on the last quarter of measure 16 and the fourth eighth-note of measure 26. The only question is, what is the best way, in both cases, to return to the great-manual. Some players already carry the tenor over to the great on the second eighth in measure 20. Others remain through measures 20 and 21 on the second manual, which they have reinforced at the beginning of measure 20 by opening the swell or by drawing additional stops, going over to the great with the soprano only at the entrance of the theme in that part, in measure 22. Even then they still keep the inner parts on the second manual, not transferring tenor and alto to the great-manual until the first quarter of measure 23. The relative convenience of these changes of manual depends on the distance between the keyboards of your particular instrument.

In measure 29 the change may be made with both hands on the second eighth before the last. But the effect is finer when only the tenor is carried over, at this point, to the great-manual, the two highest parts not following until the last eighth in the measure.

VI. Prelude and Fugue in G Minor. (Pages 20-23.)

PRELUDE

Many organists lift the last quarter-note in the first measure, for the reason that it is repeated in the following chord. But this destroys the legato connection

 required by the logic of the motive. To obtain a true legato effect, one must bind the *G* at the end of the first measure over to the chord in the second, without lifting it. Therefore, the theme should be played as if written thus:  Proceed similarly in corresponding passages.

The effect of the figurations in eighth-notes depends largely upon appropriate phrasing. This latter calls for a slight lift after the first eighth-note in the measure. In this way the listener is made aware of the construction of the period. He hears an accent on the second quarter of the measure.

Consequently, in measures 9 and 10 we should play thus:

Proceed in like manner in similar passages. When this phrasing is not observed, the piece moves rather heavily and sluggishly.

The finest effect is obtained with foundation stops, to which the mixtures of the swell-organ may perhaps be added. A change of manuals need not be taken into account.

On the fourth quarter in measure 17 a transition to a somewhat different tone-color may be made by closing the swell-box, or uncoupling the second manual, or throwing off some registers, retaining it up to the beginning of measure 23. After this, a return to the first registration is effected. By this means, not only is an agreeable variety obtained, but the development of the piece is made clearer to the listener.

FUGUE

As a matter of course, measures 1–20, 26–31 and 38–45 are to be executed on the great-organ. The episodes may be very interestingly developed by employing two manuals for their presentation. In the case of an organ with only two manuals, the great-manual can be turned into a second manual by retiring certain registers for the episodes, then using the second manual as a third. Supposing we have only a two-manual organ at our disposal, we shall, on the second quarter of measure 20, go over to the second manual with both the higher parts, remaining with the tenor on the reduced great-organ.

From the last quarter in measure 23 onward, the left hand plays the two inner parts on the second manual; the right hand goes over with the soprano to the reduced great-organ, whither the left follows on the second eighth before the last in measure 25. The stops previously retired are brought on again on the second eighth before the last in measure 26; or they may be drawn earlier, on the last quarter of the preceding measure, taking advantage of the natural *rallentando* at this point, which ought not, however, to be exaggerated.

On the second eighth in measure 31, the left hand transfers the two middle parts to the second manual; the right remains on the great, upon which, during the rest in measure 32 and the breath-pause after the first eighth-note in measure 33, stops are retired, so that the theme shall sound in a well-graduated *diminuendo*. From the second eighth before the last in measure 33 onward, the right hand takes over the two highest parts on the second manual, while the left is transferred to the reduced great-organ.

With the second eighth-note in measure 36, the right hand also returns to the great-manual. On the first beat in measure 37 a portion of the stops previously retired will be brought on again; for bringing on the remainder we shall utilize the rests in measure 38 and, if necessary, the breath-pause between the second and third eighth-notes in measure 39.

The full effect of the striking but most impressive modulations in the last two measures should be brought out by a judicious *ritenuto*.

For the employment of the swell, the following suggestions are offered: Keep it open through measures 1–20; measures 20–23 ▭ ; measures 24–25 ◁ ; through measures 26–33 it stays open; measures 34–35 ▭ ; measures 36–37 ◁ ; it then remains open till the end.

The Fugue is most effective when played with foundation stops only.

VII. Prelude and Fugue in A Minor. (Pages 24-27.)

PRELUDE

We would suggest that measures 1–11 be played on the great-manual, with foundation stops and mixtures drawn. If an augmentation be desired, add the new registers on the second sixteenth in measure 6.

Some organists play the second half of measure 2 and measure 3, and the first half of measure 5, on the second manual.

During the rest in measure 11, draw the reeds of the second manual. It will depend upon the kind of instrument at your disposal, whether the next-

following measures are played on the great or the second manual. Or, one may change from one to the other. In any event, remain on the great-manual from measure 16 onward.

FUGUE

As the pedal does not enter until near the close of the Fugue, one might feel tempted to play the entire preceding portion on the great-manual. Experience teaches, however, that in such a case the irregular construction must be taken into consideration. An episode, to be performed on the second manual, must be assumed somewhere before the entrance of the pedal; though its beginning and ending cannot be determined with precision.

We may already transfer the two highest parts to the second manual on the last eighth-note in measure 17, while leaving the left hand till (say) the second eighth-note in measure 24 on the great-manual. It is probably better to keep both hands on the great-manual as far as measure 24; then, at the end of this measure, to go over with the two highest parts to the second manual, not changing over with the tenor until the last eighth in measure 27.

In case the effect of the swell-box is so strong that the *diminuendo* of the second manual is noticeable even when its stops are combined with those of the great-organ by coupling the manuals, begin to close the swell as early as measure 20; in case the effect is distinct only when the swell is operated while you are playing on the second manual, begin the *diminuendo* only from measure 25 on.

With measure 28 the *diminuendo* should be brought to an end. Now leave the swell-box closed, up to the second half of measure 32, and from here on open it till the pedal enters.

At the end of measure 30 return with the left hand to the great-manual. On the last eighth-note in measure 34 this hand takes over the two inner parts. The soprano may be transferred back to the great-manual either on the first note in measure 35, or not until the eighth-note before the last in measure 36.

Should a closing effect be considered essential, more stops may be added at the entrance of the theme in measure 43.

It is extremely difficult to express the phrasing by notation-marks; for there is hardly any method of suitably indicating the insensible "lift" between the third eighth-note and the following dotted note in the second measure. Yet it is solely by this effect of touch, and not by a smooth binding, that one can create the illusion of a thematic accent, such as the structure of this peculiarly Bach-like tone-line calls for, on the fourth eighth-note in this measure.

This fugue, like the one preceding, appears to have been conceived for a well-chosen chorus of foundation stops.

VIII. Prelude and Fugue in B♭ Major. (Pages 28-31.)

PRELUDE

The first section sounds best when played with foundation stops and mixtures; but reeds may also be added. For the pedal solo one should probably employ the full organ.

Play the second section with foundation stops only for the first time; for the repeat add mixtures, and possibly a few reeds.

In measures 14–25 the effect depends chiefly on a correct binding and articulation of the inner parts, so that the resultant chord-successions may come out in transparent and plastic rhythm, without smothering the figurations in the highest part.

The registers to be added for the repeat of the second section can be drawn during the pedal solo in measure 24, even should the manuals be coupled to the pedal. If the successive reinforcements of stops be introduced cleverly, a fine *crescendo* in the pedal solo will result. But there are players who prefer, as a matter of principle, not to bring on the new registers until the first eighth-note of the repeat, and then all together.

FUGUE

With respect to the phrasing of the theme, opinions are divided. Some players will prefer to play the broken sixths in this way:

Still, it cannot be denied that the Bach tone-line then loses something of its characteristic, austere beauty.

This becomes especially manifest in the closing measures of the Fugue, where the theme sounds above the repeated chords. When one plays it, in this passage, with the more striking phrasing given at first, it dominates the chords; when one phrases it simply in the natural measure-rhythm, it is almost covered up by them.

Repeated experiments in playing the fugue through with either style of phrasing are likely to fix the player's choice on the first.

In this case we again plead for a pedantically correct observance of the *legato*, and of the "lifts" in the chord-successions.

We hardly need remark that the phrasing of the theme must not be over-prominent, but is merely to be indicated within the general *legato*.

Begin on the great-manual with foundation stops and mixtures, and remain upon it up to measure 25; do not hold down the chord at the beginning of this measure for its full note-value, but lift it a trifle early, and at the same time let the right hand go over to the second manual with the second eighth-note in the alto. The right hand will not follow till the second eighth in measure 28.

During the succeeding measures let the swell-box close, but so slowly that the *diminuendo* shall come to an end only in measure 35.

On the third quarter of measure 36 the soprano goes over to the great-manual; the two inner parts follow after the rests in measure 39. Up to this point, the swell-box has opened again.

The player who cannot forbear drawing additional stops toward the close of a fugue should do so, in this case, on the last quarter of measure 45, in a dignified and seemly manner.

————————————

EIGHT LITTLE PRELUDES AND FUGUES

Prepare { U B♭ ⑩ 00 7717 112
P 64 }

I
Prelude and Fugue in C Major

Edited by
Charles-Marie Widor
and Albert Schweitzer

Johann Sebastian Bach

II
Prelude and Fugue in D Minor

Prepare { U B♭ 00 7817 112
L B♭ 00 8776 432
P 67

III
Prelude and Fugue in E Minor

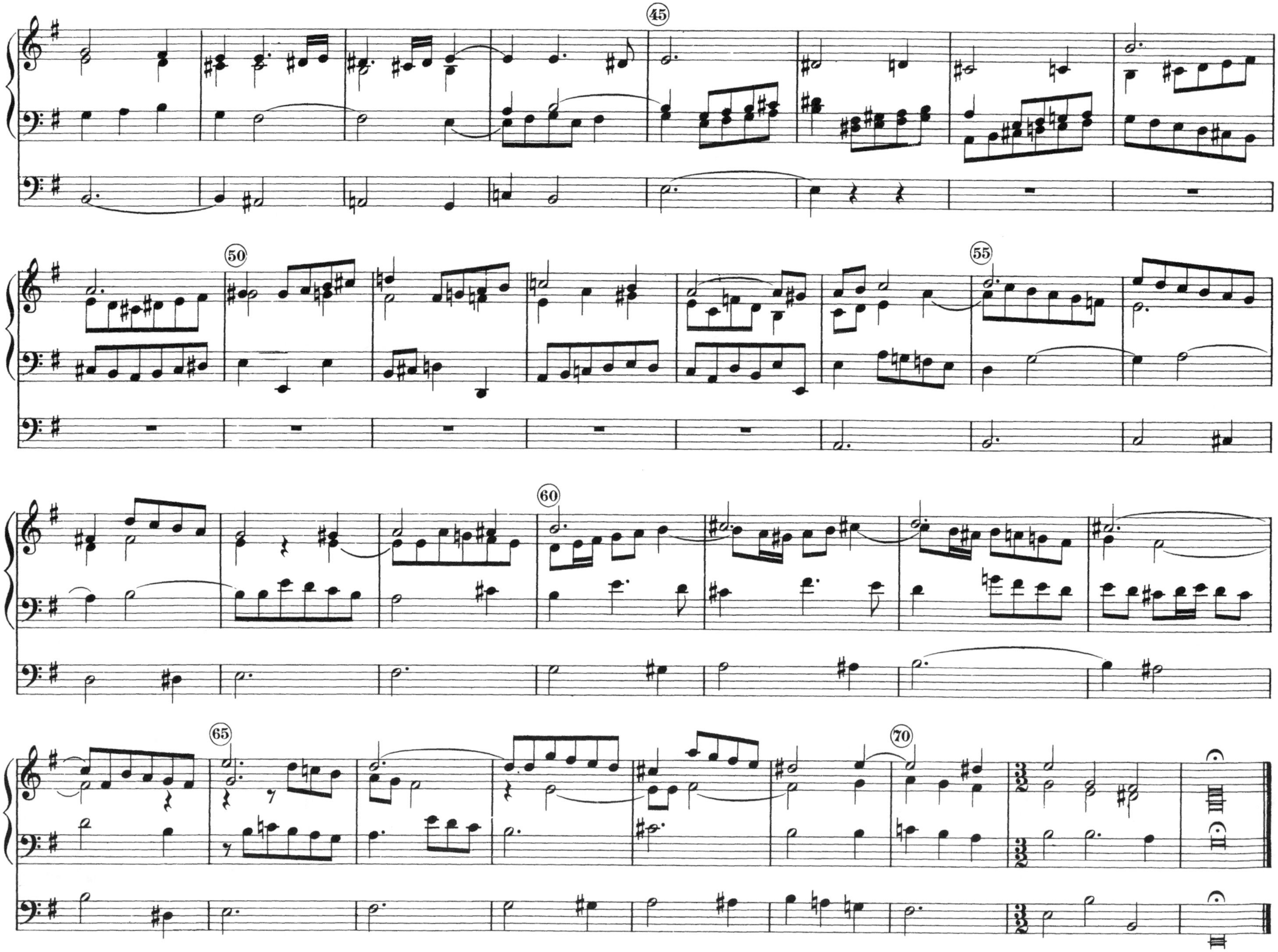
45
50
55
60
65
70

IV
Prelude and Fugue in F Major

Fugue

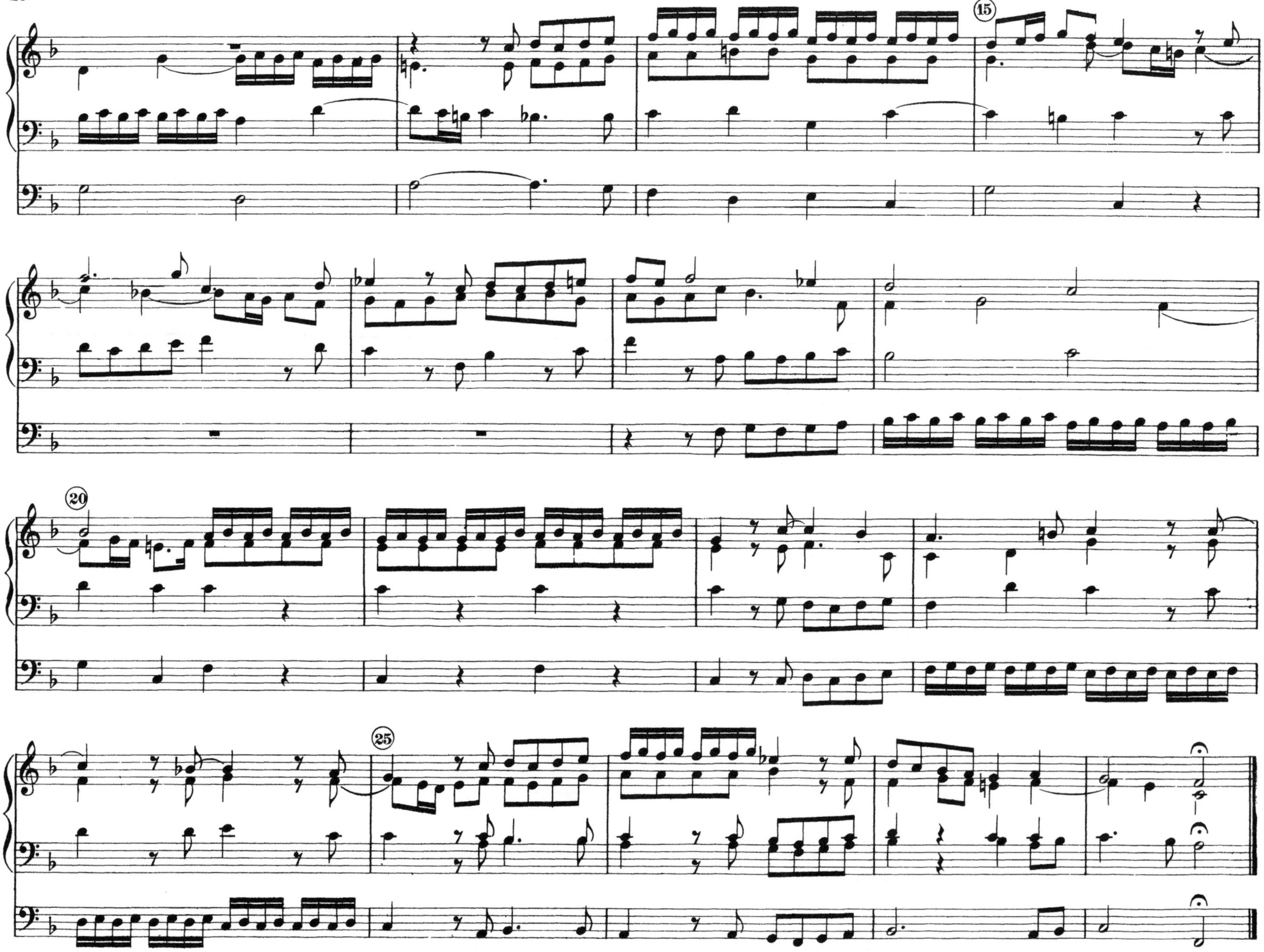
15
20
25

Prepare {U B♭ ⑩ 00 7857 345
{P 86

V
Prelude and Fugue in G Major

Prelude
Grave

(Allegro)

Manual

L A ⑨

Pedal

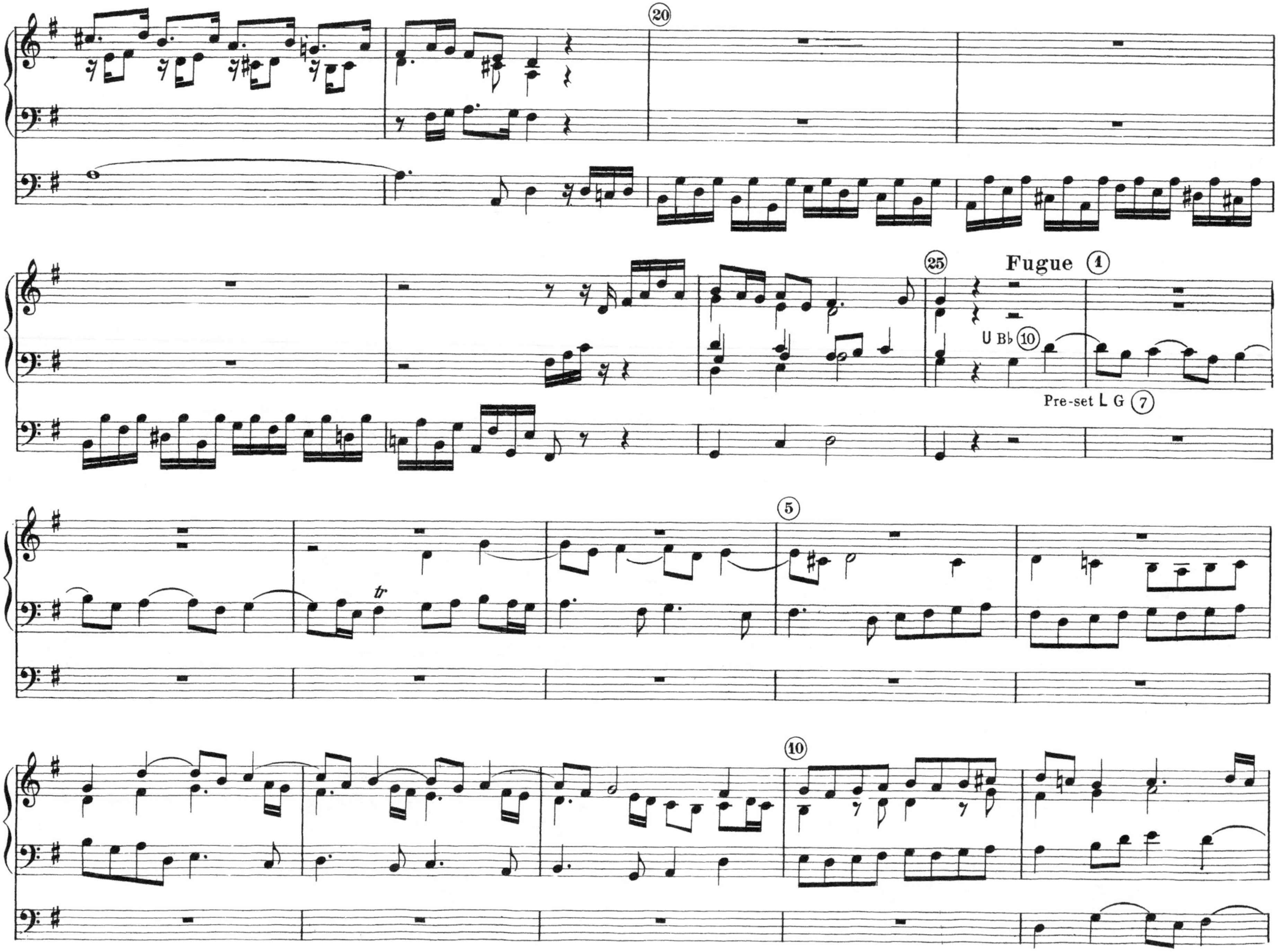
20
25
Fugue
1
U B♭ 10
Pre-set L G 7
tr
5
10

VI
Prelude and Fugue in G Minor

Fugue

VII
Prelude and Fugue in A Minor

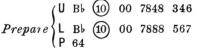

VIII
Prelude and Fugue in B Flat Major

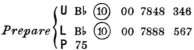

Fugue